In Search of Self

THE DIARY OF AN ADOPTEE

BRIYELL JONES

authorHOUSE®

AuthorHouse™ UK
1663 Liberty Drive
Bloomington, IN 47403 USA
www.authorhouse.co.uk
Phone: UK TFN: 0800 0148641 (Toll Free inside the UK)
UK Local: (02) 0369 56322 (+44 20 3695 6322 from outside the UK)

© 2023 Briyell Jones. All rights reserved.

No part of this book may be reproduced, stored in a retrieval system, or transmitted by any means without the written permission of the author.

This book is a non-fictional narrative based on true-life events. All names have been changed to protect the identity and privacy of the individuals involved.

Published by AuthorHouse 05/19/2023

ISBN: 978-1-7283-9313-1 (sc)
ISBN: 978-1-7283-9314-8 (e)

Print information available on the last page.

Any people depicted in stock imagery provided by Getty Images are models, and such images are being used for illustrative purposes only.
Certain stock imagery © Getty Images.

This book is printed on acid-free paper.

Because of the dynamic nature of the Internet, any web addresses or links contained in this book may have changed since publication and may no longer be valid. The views expressed in this work are solely those of the author and do not necessarily reflect the views of the publisher, and the publisher hereby disclaims any responsibility for them.

Contents

Acknowledgements vii

1	A Brief Encounter	1
2	Background History	3
3	The Early Years	4
4	Changing Faces	12
5	New Beginnings	17
6	Trust vs Mistrust	19
7	Life and Loss	24
8	Bad Education	28
9	Setting Goals	30
10	Conversations with Grandma	35
11	Baby Talk	38
12	The Break-In	40
13	Escapism	42
14	Hit-and-Miss	45
15	The Breakdown	49
16	A New Lease of Life	52
17	The Calling	54

Acknowledgements

To God, my children, nephew, and nieces.

A Brief Encounter

1987

BRIYELL WAS HAPPY TO SEE HER AFTER ALL THESE YEARS. TO BE WITHIN arm's reach of her, touch her, hear her voice, and most importantly, be in the same room as her, even if it was only for a few hours. She marvelled at the sight of her. She was 5 foot 7 tall, slender, and soft-spoken. Her piercing brown eyes complimented her golden-brown complexion. She wore her hair out and her curl patterns danced each time she moved. Her oval-shaped face was unblemished, and she had small features. She wore high-waisted jeans and a black polo neck with long sleeves. Every so often, she would hold the sleeves as if she were nervous or cold. She was told to take a seat in the living room.

Briyell's foster mum Joy called her into the kitchen. She handed her a patty that had been repurchased from Barbados; it was steaming hot and smelt delicious. She took the plate, proudly walked into the dining room, and handed it to her biological mother. She said, 'thank you,' and dug straight in. It was like she had not eaten in a while! Realising she had forgotten her drink, she rushed back to the kitchen to get it. Before swiftly leaving the kitchen, Joy stopped her in her tracks and asked, 'Briyell, how do you feel?' 'Happy!' she promptly replied and sped off, spilling some of the drink in the process. 'It was cool having two mums,' she thought as she dashed back into the living room, handing mum her drink. When her mum had finished, Briyell took the plate and glass back into the kitchen. Joy snatched the items from her and abruptly threw them in the bin. Briyell was gobsmacked! Joy then turned to her mother and scowled in her Bajan accent, 'muh nah wah catch nain!' Briyell did not understand her response as she felt that washing up liquid did a good job at keeping germs away.

She walked back into the front room, where Brandon was sitting on their mum's lap. She asked Briyell to join them. She was ecstatic! Cradling them in her arms, she sang Jackson Five's number one hit 'I Want You Back,' and she sounded beautiful. Briyell felt she was singing to them, and the song was symbolic; she kept repeating, 'Oh baby, give me one more chance' as if asking them to do just that. She then stopped, asked to use the toilet, and went taking her handbag with her.

She was a while; Briyell felt like going to check on her but never did. Suddenly, the toilet flushed, and the door swung open! As she came downstairs, she did not seem the same, and she looked disoriented and drowsy. Eventually, she made her way into the living room and slumped into the blue sofa. To Briyell's horror, she noticed some holes in her wrists; she wore a long sleeve top, so she could only imagine the entire arm. It was disturbing! She remembered earlier when she was holding her sleeves; it wasn't because she was nervous or cold. She was trying to hide the state of her arms. She had gone to the bathroom for a quick fix; To inject a dose of heroin. 'Was seeing us too much for her?' Briyell thought fearfully yet hoping that she would get back to 'normal.' Once Joy saw the state she was in, she asked her to leave. This was upsetting, and part of Briyell wanted to go with her, but she could not even look after herself. This was the last time Briyell saw her biological mother, but she hoped to see her again one day. She never really spoke to Joy about how this made her feel. She internalised a lot and put on a facade that everything was fine.

Background History

BRIYELL'S BIOLOGICAL MOTHER WAS BORN IN NEWPORT, IN 1956. SHE was of mixed parentage. Her mother was White British, and her father was Black, but his ethnic origin was unknown. Furthermore, she was unaware of who her parents were as she had been given up for adoption early and was refused any information by her foster carers, with who she was placed between the ages of 4-16. Growing up, it must have been hard for her; she did not know her immediate family, and Briyell did not know if she had any siblings. She lived independently in and around South London in her early thirties, where she met Briyell's father.

Briyell's father was black with light skin. He was of average height, always well-groomed, and a bit of a lady's man. He was born in London in 1957 but was sent to live in Barbados as an infant and brought up by his grandparents, who he was very fond of. He returned to his biological mother in England at the age of 10 and was unaware of who his father was. He also lived independently in and around South London in his early twenties, where he met Briyell's mother.

Briyell's parents had no form of physical or emotional attachment at a critical stage of childhood. They both came from broken homes with no family structure or routine. They both had to find their own way in life from an early age, which led her to believe that this was one of the first factors that affected her and her brother's childhood.

The Early Years

1980

BRIYELL WAS BORN 13 WEEKS PREMATURE AND WAS THE SECOND TWIN by two minutes. Her father, who was then 23, learnt of their birth a day later and already had a daughter from a previous relationship. And a year later, he had another daughter from another relationship. He never lived with Briyell's mother, and they were both unmarried. However, they lived in the same block of flats at one point and had history. He was said to have visited his twins a few times in hospital; though there were no records of this, he later played an active role.

There were various medical complications following Briyell's and Brandon's birth due to their mum's drug and alcohol abuse during pregnancy. Two days after their birth, their mum absconded from the hospital, and her whereabouts were unknown. She visited them occasionally, but the visiting pattern was poor and inconsistent. She also failed to contact the ward anytime she had not visited. Concerns around her drug use and possibly criminal offences were a major issue unless adequate provisions were made for her to be supervised. At the time, they needed regular check-ups at the hospital, and it was not certain that she would follow up these routine appointments. A case conference was held, and recommendations were made. In the face of all efforts made by the numerous agencies involved to help and engage their mum in all plans to move forward, it appeared she showed very little interest in their welfare.

In Search of Self

Three months later, they were discharged from the hospital and placed with foster carers. Their Mum was fully involved in this transition and accompanied them to this placement alongside social workers. There were no restrictions on her visiting them at this home, but she did not always take this up and visited three weeks after their arrival. Here, she was notified of their ongoing health issues and hospital appointments, but following this visit, she made no further attempt to see them after that, and by 1981 she was remanded in prison on four accounts of theft. Despite this, social services' plan was to rehabilitate them back to their mum as soon as possible.

1981

Halfway through the year, they returned to the care of their mother, who had been transferred to a drug rehabilitation centre from prison. She lived here for two months and was adamant about getting the help she needed to overcome her addiction. Six months into the programme, she was making progress and responded well to her children. However, this was short-lived. She relapsed, and her use of drugs became more pronounced; she no longer complied with the staff at the centre and eventually was served with a notice to leave. They then moved to an emergency family unit for a week and then to a family centre for about another week, which again broke down due to her unwillingness to co-operate with the services and inability to meet her children's needs.

She often left them unattended in their cots, unstimulated and crying for long periods. At times they were found on the floor with small objects such as plastic bags and matches. Their mum had no idea about their dietary needs; the milk and food she fed them was not age-appropriate, and they both suffered from diarrhoea at the unit. After a while, their mum informed the department that she was unwell and could not cope with them. Arrangements were made for the twins to be temporarily removed from her care until she was physically fit to have them back; however, this did not actualise. She withdrew herself from them and the department entirely.

Briyell and Brandon were then situated with an Indian family for the next two years. Their primary carer's name was Mrs. Ramah. She was a short lady, four feet tall, quite round, and spoke with a soft tone. Her long silky black hair was often worn in a plaited ponytail, and she would dress in the prettiest saris. She lived in a block of flats with her two sons and loved to cook daily for her family. The house always smelt of delicious Asian food and spices, and they enjoyed eating her meals. They were taught to pray before eating and throughout specific times of the day, and Briyell remembers kneeling on a mat each time they did so. She would take them to and from nursery and took good care of them overall. She also taught them how to speak Urdu or Hindi, but the dialect Briyell could not remember. Mrs. Ramah went on holiday for 6-8 weeks, so a temporary placement was found until her return.

1982

An assessment was carried out to determine if extended family members could be considered potential carers, including their dad. Their dad's mum was contacted and stated she could not commit to looking after them due to her work duties, and there were no extended family members on their mums' side to put forward as possible carers. One of the conference outcomes was to assess their dad's commitment to them through regular contact visits at a family centre. These visits went well, and he would sometimes bring their older sister, who was three and a half at the time, along to see them. They loved spending time together and cried whenever they would leave. Sometime after, their dad was granted open access twice a week. On Tuesday's he would collect them from Mrs Ramah's house and take them back to his house,

In Search of Self

and on Fridays, he would take them to the family centre for planned, supervised activities. He did his best to ensure their needs were met but later told the department that he could not look after them himself.

That same year social services were informed that their mum had been sentenced to 18 months' imprisonment. She had made several requests to see them whilst on remand and had written once during that time. Her requests had been refused as she had made little effort to stick to contact arrangements when she was in the community. She would turn up at their foster carer's house after they had gone to bed or five minutes before contact was due to end. It was not conducive for their routine, and there were signs of them regressing. The department felt that contact would not be in the children's best interest, so all requests for further contact were denied. Their dad also had a range of charges against him at this point but continued to have open supervised contact with them at the centre and his home. Child protection was made aware, and the visits were stopped as he was later charged and received a five-year custodial sentence.

1984

The children's paternal cousin Terrance had recently met and married his wife Joy in the Bahamas. They had a daughter and together came to live in the UK. They both later approached the department and asked to be assessed as the twin's future carers. Their biological parents had given their full support to the Social's decision to place them there, which was clarified in a full-court hearing.

Today Briyell and Brandon were getting ready to leave Mrs. Ramah's house. Teary-eyed, they trudged downstairs to the car where Joy was waiting for them. Mrs. Ramah opened the rear door of the car and safely placed both children in their seats. Leaning in, she gave each of them a kiss on their forehead; with this, they both began to cry. She closed the door, then walked over to the driver's side and told Joy to take good care of them. As the car drove off, Briyell's eyes followed Mrs. Ramah until she lost sight of her completely. The thought of moving home was frightening, as was the idea of having a new family. However, the advantage of this move would provide them with a family placement, meet their racial and cultural needs, and offer them contact with their extended family members.

Soon they pulled onto the drive of their new home and were introduced to a lady called Aunt Leah, with who they would also be living with. It was a four-bedroom house with a neat little garden. They showed them around, then sat and ate dinner together. They tried to settle the children down for bed a while later, but they stayed up the whole night; thinking they were returning home to Mrs. Ramah. Eventually, they fell asleep in the early hours of the next day. Saturday morning, they were up early, and Briyell was speaking the native tongue of her foster carer. Joy called Mrs. Ramah, who told her that Briyell wished to use the toilet. Laughter filled the room as Joy relayed the information back to their relatives.

Developmentally, Briyell was a little more advanced than Brandon, though they both had speech and language delay. Briyell could walk and was fully toilet trained, whilst Brandon was a working progress. He also needed regular check-ups at the hospital, which Joy would always accompany him to. He suffered from daily nose bleeds and head-banging temper tantrums, and Briyell would scream out in her sleep and suffer from nightmares. An open line of communication was kept between Joy and Mrs. Ramah for a short while to suit their needs and security.

The next day, Joy had picked up their younger sister from her mum's house and together went to visit their dad in prison. He had only done a year out of the five of which he got sentenced. They were excited when they saw him, and Briyell was sure he felt the same way. She was most surprised to see that he had made the girls stuffed teddies and Brandon a red and white ball. He and Joy spoke for a while, and he was thrilled that they were now placed in her care. They had fun on these visits. Leaving was the difficult part. Brandon would cling to his dad, not wanting to go, which was upsetting for all of them. It was hard seeing someone they love behind bars and not be able to do anything about it!

Their biological mother was still imprisoned at this point. Joy had taken them to see her three times, and she would write otherwise. When released, she was issued supervised visits to see her children four times a year, namely Easter, Summer, birthdays, and Christmas. Briyell got so excited when these visits came around but devastated when she never showed up. However, there was one visit that she did remember. About a year before the brief encounter, Joy had taken them to a house where their mum was staying. At the door, Briyell stood anxious, thinking she would not show, but she did! As her mum opened the door, she had a big smile on her face. Briyell charged towards her and held her tightly, like a boa constrictor choking its prey. She did not want to let go! Her mum handed her a pink and yellow microphone and a plastic sound tube toy that she was fascinated with. Each time Briyell tipped the tube upside-down, she mimicked the sound of the groaning toy. There was a small garden with a few shabby toys. Briyell and Brandon made the most of them whilst Joy and their mum spoke. Impatiently Briyell came back inside, and Brandon followed. She shyly shuffled towards her mum and huddled around her; this closeness was everything! There were things Briyell wanted to ask her, like – 'when would she get them back?' and 'when her next visit would be?' but didn't as she thought it might have made Joy uncomfortable. The meeting ended in a flash, 'I wish time could stand still,' Briyell thought at that moment. They kissed and hugged each other goodbye and looked forward to more meetings like this.

Briyell Jones

1984

Terrence and Joy had now been approved as the children's long-term foster carers. They taught them about 'family' and felt they had a part to play in helping them challenge racism and develop positive identities as black children in society. One evening Joy was baking in the kitchen, and they were hovering around her feet as usual. She looked at them and randomly asked, 'children, what colour are you?' 'White,' they uncannily answer. She told them they were black and demonstrated this by mixing a cup of hot chocolate. First, she put a spoonful of coco into a cup and said, 'this is your father,' then, whilst pouring the milk, she would say, 'this is your mother!'. They marvelled as they saw the mixture combine. Then she would firmly say, 'you are this!' referring to the now light brown mixture in the cup. Joy repeated this daily and reiterated, 'you guys are Black children; what colour are you?' 'Black!' they shot back as if being in a rapid-fire round question quiz.

Joy was the closest mother-figure Briyell had growing up. She was ambitious and hardworking. At the time, Joy was studying at university and tried her best to make ends meet. She taught them how to pray before they ate and before going to bed. They learnt how to set a dinner table and how to use a knife and fork. When it came to their learning, she did not play around! She taught them how to write their names and how to count. She often got angry when Briyell got questions wrong and would punish her for this. She was a bit more lenient with Brandon as he had learning difficulties. Nonetheless, she taught them the same things.

Another fond memory Briyell has as a child growing up is when her aunt Leah came home with a personalised book titled 'African American Heroes' that depicted Martin Luther King's Journey through the Civil Rights Movement. She loved having it read to her and found comfort in this book. It gave her hope that one day she would be able to make a change. So now, the children embraced their British culture,

In Search of Self

learnt about black history, and identified with their Caribbean origins. They had another aunt who was good at drawing Disney characters to the point where Briyell wondered if she was the animator of Walt Disney. Her art was just that good! These pictures were hung in their bedroom, which made it more child-friendly and fun. They grew happy in this home and had come a long way from where they were. They attended nursery and were achieving age-appropriate milestones; their behaviour had improved, and they were also secure in having contact with their extended family, but unfortunately, like all good things, it came to an end!

1986

Joy had come to a difficult decision that she could no longer care for the twins on a full-time basis. She was experiencing difficulties in her marriage which eventually broke down. However, she still showed an interest in pursuing their adoption in her own rights, but it would take some time due to the circumstances. Contact with their extended family was also ceased. Briyell was angry and did not want to be moved again, and from her knowledge, no other family members tried to help. She did not even know if any family knew of the separation and guessed they had their own lives to worry about. There was nothing she could do or say to change the situation. She felt alone and had nobody to talk to except Brandon, and he was just as frustrated and fed up as she was. They were then moved to alternative foster parents for a week, and due to lack of space, moved to another carer for another week then spent three months with another carer. This was an extremely emotional and difficult time for them. They were distressed and kept asking to go back to live with Joy.

Changing Faces

1986

EARLY THAT YEAR, A DECISION WAS MADE, AND BRANDON AND BRIYELL returned to Joy's care. As far as they were concerned, they were home! They continued to attend the same school, but there were still a lot of issues. Their dad had been released from prison, and he visited them regularly to start with, but his inconsistency and lack of support often caused arguments between him and Joy. They visited their mum once at prison whilst she was there, and to say the least, it negatively impacted them, and their behavioural problems continued. All further contact with their mum had been ceased as a result of this. Social services regularly visited the house to monitor their situation, and six months into the placement, Joy could no longer manage, and the placement broke down again.

Later that year, they moved to a foster carer called Cynthia. Whilst the move was distressing for them, Briyell adapted to her lifestyle, which was okay, apart from sharing a bed with three other adoptees, one who would occasionally wet the bed. His name was Martin. This was the first time they had been in foster care with other children, and Briyell found it strange that she had to share a bed with more than one child, especially boys. She kept to herself and tried not to get in anyone's way. Joy maintained contact with them during this period which helped to some extent, but their behaviour was still problematic.

In Search of Self

This placement lasted one week due to lack of space, but boy, were they happy to leave. Their biological parents were aware of the move. Their father had visited them twice at this placement, and their birth mother was still imprisoned.

1987

A year later, they moved back to Joys, where they stayed for another five months. Briyell now attended regular meetings with a psychologist to discuss her feelings and experiences. She found it nice having one-to-one time with someone that seemed to care about how she felt. But most times wasn't always willing to co-operate in the sessions or tell the truth, for that matter. Sometimes the meetings felt intrusive, and she felt like a subject rather than a child. At the same time, she and Brandon were being prepared to move to another foster carer called Jocelyn, who was of Jamaican origin. She was dark-skinned with a smooth complexion. Her hair was twisted in locks with silver foil on the ends; Jocelyn was of medium build, had a good dress sense and a warm smile. She was married to a man named Beryl, who was tall, dark, and mean-looking! On the day, Joy drove with them to their new home. They got out of the car, bags in hand and rang the doorbell. The carers buzzed them in, and they made their way upstairs. Briyell was nervous. Her heart rate increased, her legs trembled with every step, and her stomach churned. Jocelyn stood at the top of the hallway and introduced herself. Briyell's nerves slowly eased. They all went into the kitchen and briefly discussed the new living arrangements, and once Joy was happy, she told them they would be okay and left.

Days turned to weeks and weeks into months, and they adapted. Beryl was not all that bad; he was a big softy under all that muscle. Whenever Briyell and Brandon did wrong, they were made to stay

Briyell Jones

in their bedrooms, and their favourite toys were taken away. Their new primary school was a five-minute walk from home. Joycelyn attended school meetings and was generally there for them overall. Often, Jocelyn took the twins to visit her friend Sophie who had three children of her own; Jade, Jayson and Erwin and together would play around the estate. Jade, Sophie's eldest daughter, was stunning. She was black, beautiful, and popular. Briyell looked up to Jade as a big sister and enjoyed spending time with her. Jade always took Briyell out and about with her. One day they visited her friend's house. Music was the topic of discussion, and then Jade started to sing. Briyell's jaw dropped to the floor as she heard her angelic tones. A while later, they ate, laughed, and spoke some more. When Jade got back to her house, Briyell shyly explained that she too could sing. 'Really! Sing for me then?' she requested, but Briyell was too shy and refused. She was around 9 or 10 when she realised this gift, and music has always been a part of her.

As time went on, Briyell began playing up in school, demanding attention by being disruptive, lying, stealing and other wrongdoings. Joy continued to visit Briyell at this placement and often encouraged them to behave. One Christmas, Joy visited and told Jocelyn she was taking them out to get ice cream, but they ended up at her house. Christmas time was the best at Joy's house. The tree was always beautifully decorated, and the ceilings in every room were draped with tinsel. Their stockings were always stuffed with chocolates and sweets, and together, they would write letters to Santa and leave milk and cookies out for him. It felt jolly good to be back, thought Briyell! They opened their presents and ate dinner with all the trimmings. It felt like they had never left! 'If anybody asks... tell them we went for ice cream,' Joy instructed. They agreed to stick to this story, but out of excitement, they told Joycelyn everything. Trouble is what they were in, and Joy was issued a warning.

1989

Months flew by, and Briyell and Brandon were still showing signs of unwanted behaviour, which later got them moved to residential care, a children's home where they stayed for 11 months. Their clothes had been packed, and a white van man picked them up. On route, Briyell became anxious. They were driving further away, and she no longer recognised her surroundings. When they arrived at the home, it was one of the biggest they had ever seen. 'What if I get lost?' Briyell thought worryingly. They were greeted by a few of the workers and shown their bedrooms. Surprisingly, Briyell had her own room. The first night, however, was scary, and she found it difficult to sleep. The thought of someone entering her room played on her mind, as well as now living in a house with complete strangers. As time went on, the home was not at all that bad.

Briyell attended the same Primary School as she did whilst living with Joycelyn, and Brandon still attended his school. Briyell was dropped off in a minibus every day without fail. This was a little embarrassing, and she was often teased and bullied by the other children about this. Some children would say, 'What … your mum and dad can't afford to look after you?'. 'You guys are orphans!', others taunted. Briyell tried not to take notice, but their words cut deep. They were given weekly pocket money based on good behaviour and if their weekly chores were completed, but still, there was no improvement in their behaviour. Brandon would get restrained regularly, which made Briyell angry because, in those moments, it looked like more harm was being done, and Brandon's screams for help broke her heart.

On the other hand, Briyell was often verbally abusive, disobedient, and continued to lie and steal, which she often got sanctioned for. Once, she lied about not seeing out of her right eye properly and having no knowledge that this would require further inspection. Her key worker booked an optician appointment. Briyell faked the eye chart test, and after a while, June realised that she had made the whole thing up. Briyell got sanctioned and was banned from every child-related activity. Although this was for her good, and through it, she should have been learning a valuable lesson, she disliked the punishment, and it showed in her behaviour at school.

Briyell and Brandon's key workers were called on regularly for meetings with their teachers, and after a while, the staff began to call their dad to ask if he could come up with strategies of 'discipline' for them. This would result in them getting beaten and told to behave. The staff knew about this but guess they had given up and thought this was the final solution. Soon after, Briyell's key worker started working closely with her; it was something she needed. As she began to appreciate things, she was rewarded with swimming trips, bowling, cinemas, and other child-friendly activities. She also had joined 'Brownies' and enjoyed trampolining. This remained consistent throughout the rest of their stay at the Children's Home.

As months passed, their dad expressed an interest in fostering them, which became one of the home's focal points. It started with daily visits and gradually extended to overnight weekend stays. He registered them in a local youth club and took them on trips with their sisters. Although none of them ever lived with him on a permanent basis, he would ensure all his children had contact one way or another.

New Beginnings

1990

UNDER SECTION 31 OF THE CHILDREN ACT 1989, A FULL CARE ORDER was issued, which meant that the twins would be placed with their dad on a full-time basis. The family home was a three-bedroom house. Briyell's room was big and had been painted purple. Brandon had a small box room that was painted blue. 'How cliché,' Briyell thought typically. She had mismatched bed sheets and curtains; nonetheless, this was home. Months later, their dad had taken them to Barbados for four weeks. It allowed them to establish a closer relationship with him and his extended family. Briyell met all her cousins and loved going out with them. Every day was something new. She learnt a lot on this trip, especially about the family unit; it was strong, everyone looked out for everyone, something she thought was rare in the UK. Sadly, it was time to return home. However, she was happy to go back to school and shared her holiday experience. She also thought it would be a good time to buckle down as she was now in her final year of Primary school. She learnt she would be attending a Secondary school for girls and that Brandon would attend a school that catered for his special needs. She was hopeful that he would get the support he needed after all these years.

Every day, Briyell would take the train partway with her dad, walk the rest of the journey to school and make her way to his workplace after school. His workplace was always busy and had been known to a few celebrities. Sometimes, Briyell would help clean up at the end of each day. She always found the topics of conversation interesting in the shop. They were on things such as politics, religion, culture, music and women. She particularly enjoyed going there on the weekends. Her dad allowed her and her brother to go to the park independently, and after, they would buy chicken and chips for lunch and treat themselves to penny sweets at the corner shop.

Trust vs Mistrust

THIS WAS ROUTINE FOR AT LEAST A YEAR AND A HALF UNTIL THEIR DAD put his trust in them to start going straight home after school. He put them in a cab and had instructed them to carry out certain chores, which had to be completed before he got home. After a while, these chores were neglected, and they would do what most children do. Watch TV, play games and not care about what their dad had told them to do. Their dad soon put a stop to this and reminded them with a back slap that 'slipping'- not listening was out of the question.

In the meantime, their dad remained patient with them until he grew weary from their behaviour. This was soon settled as he used the West Indian method of discipline. They dealt with this by 'padding up.' They would wear about three pairs of trousers and five tops to avoid feeling the pain. Their dad's motto was, 'If you can't hear, you must feel!' which he meant literally. He would use almost anything insight or on him like his belt, a hanger, his hands, feet, or air freshener bottles. Sometimes it did not matter how many clothes they had on; he would drag them off and carry on with this method of discipline.

Joy would do the same; they both grew up with this type of discipline instilled in them. Funny enough, she would use terms for her, ones like 'The Duck.' When they would misbehave, she would roll her fist up in a ball and ask, 'Do you want a duck?' This was a punch on the arm or wherever she could land one. They would tense their bodies up or run at the mere mention of it. Other times she would send them to stand facing a corner and told them to hold one leg up and place the opposite hand over their head. Strangely, Briyell preferred this method as there was no direct pain apart from her arms tiring from the position of standing and trying to balance. Both twins hated these types of punishment, but to both parents, it was a way of teaching their children that if they did something wrong, they would be punished. Guess they had to learn one way or the other!

Throughout the different years of Briyell and Brandon's schooling, a range of safeguarding concerns were raised whilst living with their dad and Joy. Sometimes they had got beaten, and the marks were visible. Some they hid, and others they did not. Briyell was in her PE lesson one afternoon but sat on the side-lines contemplating whether to join in. She had to wear shorts that would reveal the belt mark she got the night before. The belt mark was visible, and she was still in a lot of pain. 'If anyone asks you about it, tell them you fought with your brother,' her dad instructed. 'Briyell, are you not joining in?' her teacher asked. Briyell froze and did not know what to say. One side of her wanted to show the teacher what her dad had done, and the other side wanted to protect him, but she really wanted the beatings to stop. She plucked up the courage and decided to show the teacher the belt wound on her thigh. Shocked is what she was and immediately raised a safeguarding concern. Briyell did not tell anyone about the beatings before this part because she believed she deserved it and was used to it. If she were told not to do something and did it anyway, she knew a beating would be heading her way, and that was exactly how she felt now that her teacher knew. She worried about the consequence of her actions and thought she had made things worse.

After school, she slowly made her way to her dads' workplace. Once there, she opened the door and walked hastily into the back of the shop, flinching past him as she went by. She and Brandon spoke about their day events. Coincidently, he had also informed his teacher about his dad's mistreatment. Briyell was relieved in a way that it was not all on her. They had both got it off their chests. It must have been a twin thing! After the investigation, social services thought it be best if Briyell was moved into the care of a positive female. She went back to live with Joy, and Brandon stayed with his dad. Apart from their initial separation in their early years, this was the longest time they had been apart from each other. Briyell found it strange, though part of her was missing. She was anxious, and a feeling of loneliness came over her. She no longer had her brother to mother, to talk and laugh with in good times or bad, and she wondered if he felt the same.

Joy had remarried, birthed her own twins, and Briyell was now living with them in their family home. Briyell found it strange seeing Joy with her newfound family as it had once been them like this. Feelings of jealousy would arise but would be surpassed by love and compassion. Briyell was totally besotted with their new-born babies and enjoyed watching them, care and nurture them. Her relationship with Joy's husband was good. He was cool, calm, and collected. Briyell would wash and iron her clothes and sometimes prepare her meals. There were times when Joy would call her into the kitchen to help her prepare dinner. As she would help, Joy would say, 'Look, you can't even peal a potato; your cousin can peel them ten times better than you.' She compared Briyell's abilities to others quite a lot which Briyell hated. Whenever Briyell tried to explain how this made her feel, Joy would say she had an attitude and shut her down completely. This happened frequently, and Briyell felt that she could not express herself because of this. She took the bus to and from school every morning. One morning Briyell boarded the bus to school, a boy her age sat next to her. 'What music you into?' he asked her. 'I like R&B,' she replied, and he handed her a blue CD player and told her to keep it. She was touched by this and thought nothing of it until a few weeks later.

1994

Joy booked a family holiday to Hawaii, and Briyell was elated when told she would be going with her. The flight went well, and they were picked up at the airport by Joy's sister, who they would be staying with. The family house was amazing, and the fact that it was Christmas made it even more special. Briyell met the rest of Joy's sisters' family, and they all seemed like lovely people. Later, they visited her husband's relatives and had a blast. When they arrived back home in the UK, Joy received a phone call explaining that her sister's eldest son had lost his CD player. She knew Briyell had one and questioned her about it. She then accused her of stealing it from her sister's house. Innocent, Briyell told her it had been given to her. Joy did not believe her and started lashing out; she slapped her in the face, called her a liar and beat her repeatedly. Joy said she was an embarrassment and a thief. 'Take me to the bus stop and show me this boy who gave you the CD player!' she demanded. Briyell was happy to prove her innocence, but unfortunately, the boy did not show. This angered Joy further. 'You think I'm a damn fool, ah you tek di people dem CD player, u damn thief!' There was nothing Briyell could say that would make her think differently. It was a case of the classic tale 'The boy who cried wolf,' and she was sent back to live with her dad.

Every Sunday morning at 6 am, her dad would shout from the bottom of the stairs, 'Briyell, wake up and come cook!' The first dish he taught her was rice and peas, and chicken. Each week was something new. She admired his culinary skills, as she knew one day, she would be able to cook like him or even better. However, her first attempts at Sunday dinner were a total flop, but with patience and practice, they got better. Before her dad went to work, he would lecture her and Brandon on life's dos and don'ts. This meant that when they did the opposite, their skin would pay the price. In some instances, Briyell wondered if his anger stemmed around other issues, maybe his childhood, socio and

In Search of Self

economic factors, being a single parent, who knows? But she strongly felt that there was more to it than just their behaviour.

Her biological mother was also at the forefront of her mind. She had questions she wanted to ask her, 'but how would she go about finding her?' One Saturday, she boarded the bus to an area she heard her mum was well known in and was determined to find her! She searched the market but got nothing. She then made her way to the local Police Station. On entry, she became anxious. Behind the desk, a muscular white man sat engulfed in paperwork; she slowly walked over, contemplating what to say. 'Can I help you?' he asked. She gave him her mums' name and asked if he was familiar. 'She's well known to this police station,' he replies. Elated but equally embarrassed, she asks, 'when was she last here?' 'A few weeks ago,' he confirms and gets back to his work. 'So close yet so far,' she thinks to herself and heads back home. She made several further attempts to search for her mum but had no luck finding her on either of them.

Life and Loss

1996

BRIYELL WAS IN HER PURPLE POSTER BEDROOM WATCHING TV WHEN SHE heard a loud knock at the door. She ran to the bathroom, stood on the toilet, and looked through the window. Surprisingly, it was the police. She bolted down the stairs and opened the front door. 'Is there an appropriate adult home?' one of the officers asked. 'No,' she answered, wondering if someone had reported her and her brother home alone. 'We're sorry… but we can't tell you anything until an appropriate adult is here!' She raced to call her dad, relayed back the message, and he said he would be home shortly. She thought he would take forever, so she called Joy, and in the blink of an eye, she was outside. Brandon let her in, and together with the police, they gathered in the living room.

Now with an appropriate adult at hand, they said, 'we have some bad news about your mother… she was walking down the street and was unfortunately hit in the head with an unidentified weapon. 'Is she dead?' Briyell blurted out. 'She's currently in hospital in a critical condition…. she *was* on a life support machine, but unfortunately they've had to turn it off'. Immediately Briyell zoned out. 'What if I could get to the hospital and resuscitate her?' 'Maybe if she heard my voice, she'd wake up?' Briyell thought. A sudden knock at the door snapped her out of her daydream. She figured it was her dad, so she let him in. He introduced himself, and the police repeated the brutal

In Search of Self

attack of their mother. He did not seem bothered by the news. He was probably more worried about them finding his weed stash more than anything else. Tears streamed down Briyell's face, and her heart shattered into a thousand pieces. Joy, however, was more sympathetic. She told them everything would be okay and that she would help with the funeral arrangements.

Before the funeral, Briyell prepared a speech that read, 'Even though we never knew our mum much, we still had a brief picture in the back of our minds of what she was like, and deep down we knew she was a good person. We also wished that we could have spent a couple of days with her at least, but one thing we do know is that she would have really appreciated us being here today, so let her soul rest in peace. We will always love you, mum.' On the day of the funeral, Joy, Briyell, and Brandon drove to the cemetery, found a parking space, and walked over to the church. Another funeral was taking place, so they were told to wait outside until their mum arrived. At this point, Briyell thought she would see her mum walk down the path of the cemetery to join them. It sounds strange, but she thought weird things like this to subside her pain. In fact, it was denial, one of the early stages of grief and loss. She had not really accepted the fact that her mum was gone for good! Brandon had tears in his neglected eyes. Joy held him tightly. Briyell stood on the other side of her, not wanting her emotions to get the best of her. The funeral director announced a further delay, so again they were left to wait. More people started to arrive dressed in black attire, chit-chatting amongst themselves. The director received a message, walked back over to Joy, Briyell and Brandon and told them their mum would be arriving any minute.

Briyell's palms grew sweaty, and her heart started pounding. As the black hearse drew near, Joy grasped her hand and said, 'you know Briyell, it's okay to cry!' Still, she contained her emotions and watched as the car drew closer until it stopped right in front of them. Briyell observed the pine coffin laid across the seat with pink and yellow flowers around it, and her mind began to race. 'Was mum really inside the coffin?' 'could this be staged?' she thought again in complete denial. Tears filled her eyes, and she busted out crying. She could no longer hold them back, there was a lump in her throat, and her heart was heavy. She wanted to see her mum for the last time. She expressed this to Joy, who explained that her mum's appearance would cripple her young mind due to the drugs. Still deluded, she was convinced that nothing would scare her, even if she did look like a monster from a horror movie, but Joy stuck by her word and explained that seeing her in this state was a definite no. She was not harsh; she used a soothing tone and reassured them that everything would be okay.

They entered the church, sat at the front, and the funeral commenced. The priest spoke about life and death, followed by the scriptures and a few hymns. He then announced that Briyell had a speech. She grew nervous and took to the stand... 'Even though we never knew mum much...'a few lines into the speech, her throat tightened, and tears blurred her vision. She stared at the strangers before her and her blood boiled. She felt like saying to the eight or so people in the congregation that they were only there to see what she and her brother looked like now they were grown up. Also, that they did not really care for her mum, or she would still be alive if they just took the time to help her when she really needed it. Staring into the crowd of strangers, she noticed her dad had not even attended, and this fuelled her sense of fury further. Her mind raced with uncertainties. 'What could have gone so wrong between them?' She thought. 'Surely, they must have had good times together,' but only they knew. She still felt that he should have shown up to support them regardless of what they had encountered. Eventually, she got through the rest of the speech and sat back down. The coffin was then bought out and entered a cremation chamber. Ashes to ashes dust to dust.

In Search of Self

The next morning Briyell's dad called her downstairs to wash the dishes. Whilst doing so, he asked her an odd question, 'Do you think it was me that killed her?' Puzzled, she answered 'no' but partly wanted to say yes. She knew her mother loved him, and in all the letters that her mum wrote to him, she couldn't understand why he didn't write back or even try to contact her considering he was the father of her kids. She finished the dishes, went up to her room and silently cried into her pillow. Weeks later, their mum's ashes arrived at the house, and Briyell hid them in her wardrobe. After school, she would rush home, take them out and hold them close to her. 'We were together at last, even if she was in a plastic jar,' Briyell thought. She found comfort in this and repeated this every day until it was time to scatter her ashes.

Bad Education

Year 7 – 9 in school was a breeze. Briyell was in good sets and achieving good grades for most, if not all, of her subjects. Every day after school, she would rush home to receive her dad's 4 pm phone call as instructed. She would cook and clean then call him back to ask if she and Brandon could play out. 'You clean di house properly?' he would ask. She told him she did upstairs, and Brandon did downstairs, even though she had cleaned the whole house. Whenever she would ask Brandon to help, he would get aggressive and hit her, which sometimes drew blood. She kept this to herself for years until one day, she had enough and told her dad. His response was also to act violently, so she never blamed Brandon for his temperament as children live what they learn. At school, nobody knew her past or what she was going through, and from years 9 – 11, things started to go downhill. She was now preparing for her GSCE'S and whilst she was eager to learn; she struggled to revise at home.

Every other weekend she had the responsibility of picking up and looking after her little cousin. She still had to cook and clean every day, and on top of this, she was now grieving. All of which had an impact on the time she spent on coursework and revision. Over time, she became frustrated because she was underachieving and began acting out in lessons and often got sent out or given detention. She became insecure during her school years. She did not think she was smart, attractive, or likable as some of the other girls. She would see girls with name-brand

In Search of Self

shoes and clothes and wanted to be like them. On non-uniform days, she stuck out like a sore thumb and often hid in the toilets to avoid getting bullied. She guessed that might have been why uniforms were invented to make everybody feel the same, but even so, her uniform was different from that of the other girls. She wore a second-hand uniform most of the time, none of her jumpers had the school logo on, except the one she wore in year 7, and her skirts were never fully pleated. She remembers selling crisps, chocolates, donuts, and drinks to her peers to eat a good lunch and to save to buy clothes that she liked.

Despite this, her personality helped her through school. She made people laugh, gave good advice and was good at styling hair. She was a member of the school choir, performed in talent shows and competed in athletics, which helped her confidence over the years. Sex, drugs, and rock n roll were the main topics of discussion by some girls in school. Most of her peers seemed like they had the freedom to do as they pleased. Some raved, had boyfriends and would drink and smoke. She did, however, start smoking in her last two years of school. As she took up this bad habit, she became less focused on school and her grades. When she got her exam results, they were poor, but what could she do. All she knew is that she wanted a fresh start and to make something of herself but did not know which route to take.

Setting Goals

1997

JOY ENCOURAGED HER TO GO TO COLLEGE, SO SHE ENROLLED AND attended a course that was really rewarding. She was in a good place until one evening; her dad broke some unfortunate news to her and her brother. 'We haffa go move soon you nah, cah dem people a go come tek di place.' They were being evicted! The thought of moving out of their 'family home' was daunting, so Briyell rushed to the council to seek help but got nothing. When her dad found out what she had done, he asked why. She told him she wanted to help, but he just laughed at her expense. On the other hand, she felt a pang of relief. Sure, she would have missed the house he had 'fought' for, but she told herself that everything happened for a reason.

Joy offered to let the twins stay with her good friend. She was a lovely lady with a heart of gold and helped a lot when they lived with Joy as children. Whenever they visited her in Canada, she would make sure they were well looked after. Living with her now would be a breeze; the only problem *was* Briyell had to share a room with Brandon; at 17, this was not cool! They fought about who would sleep on the bed. Brandon won, and Briyell slept on a mattress on the floor. She did not think this was right, but what else could she do. Brandon snored loud like thunder, and most nights she could not sleep. She would cook breakfast and dinner, do the food shopping and with a little

In Search of Self

financial support from their dad, they would contribute to rent, gas and electric. Joy had got them on income support; it was another solution to their state of poverty. It meant they would learn to understand the importance of money and save and spend when necessary.

1998

A few months into the stay, things were not looking good. They could not afford to live there anymore, plus there was a range of issues happening at the house. Brandon's violence towards Briyell had escalated, and he was doing whatever he wanted to do. Briyell became hostile because of this, and whenever she told Joy what had happened, Joy would shout at them and tell them to stop. There was only so much she could take, and out of anger, she said some hurtful things in the process that Briyell did not agree with. Enough was enough! Joy told them to pack their things and moved them to a nearby hostel. Briyell was taken to one which promoted independent living, and Brandon was taken to a supported sheltered hostel. They were only five minutes away from each other, so they were still able to maintain contact. Briyell was shown her room and immediately unpacked her things. She was still at college and would take the bus to and from the station every day. She was now pursuing a Diploma and became very much interested in the course, particularly the theoretical aspect. She spent time researching different theorists and how their ideas were proven. She would sometimes relate them to her own life to find reasons why she did certain things or behaved a certain way. She started to gain confidence through learning and accepting her childhood and was awarded the 'Overall Student of the Year' achievement.

She also spent a lot of time searching for her identity in star signs. She would buy moonstones, read the daily horoscopes in magazines, and often read fiction books and magazines with highly sexual content and get lost in a world of seduction and lust. At college, she had particularly grown fond of a few people. Her tutor Mariah guided and advised her on more than just her college assignments, and they had a good relationship, and Briyell often confided in her. Mariah told her if she ever were to have a daughter, she would name her Briyell. Years later, her tutor had children and stuck by her word. How sweet! A youth worker called Chi also impacted her greatly, and they generally had a good relationship.

Briyell tried to pursue one of her dreams and enrolled in a part-time music technology course. At first, she was a little apprehensive about taking on a new workload whilst studying her Diploma, but she was driven and thought it was feasible. She started the course and was fascinated by the process of engineering. One evening during class, her phone rang, she answered, but no one was there. When the class had finished, she packed up her things and left the classroom. Her phone rang again, she answered, but still nothing. She hung up and exited the college. Just then, a boy she knew jumped out of the bushes. 'Hi Bri, I've missed you…did I hug you earlier because I thought I did earlier'…? He was not making any sense and was known to have mental health issues. 'What are you doing here?' And how did you know what college I went to?' she asked, totally freaked out. She ran to the bus stop, hopped on the bus, and he followed, asking questions. She asked him to leave her alone, but he would not. Her heart was beating fast, and she did not want to make any sudden movements, as she wasn't sure what he was capable of.

Approaching her stop, she pressed the bell and shot off the bus. She looked behind and saw he was still following her. 'Leave me alone!' she shouted and ran all the way to the hostel. The next day she reported the incident to staff and police, who advised her to get a panic alarm in case it happened again. A few weeks later, she was shocked to hear her name called from a speaker in class. 'Can Briyell please report to reception immediately!'. Security guards and police were everywhere. She was

In Search of Self

rushed to an unknown part of the college. She was told that a boy had got through security and was running around the college looking for her, proclaiming that she was his dead wife. For her safety, she stopped attending the class and continued her diploma course in the daytime.

Life in a hostel was hard. One evening Briyell was in her room, thinking of ways to earn some extra money, she decided to start selling cooked food. She had flyers made and posted them in every room. She went to the £1 shop and purchased plastic containers, knives, spoons, and napkins. She bought £5 worth of chicken, a pack of basmati rice, kidney peas and some salad. That Sunday, she put it to the test. The smell of food attracted a few people who came to see what was cooking. Some bought meals, and others queried vegetarian options, which she had not considered. The staff even bought food and said it was good. This helped her with her finances and enabled her to pay her rent on time.

2000

A year or so later, she was offered a studio flat. She picked up the keys and went to view the flat. 'They *must* think I'm desperate,' she thought as she scanned the bedsit. She wondered if the council were aware of the state of their properties before giving a tenant their tenancy agreement and keys. 'Oh well,' she thought; This was home, and home is what she made it! After passing her diploma, she signed up to a local agency, worked part-time, and decided to retake her GCSE'S before going to university. Little did she know that the college was in the same area where her mum was murdered. Everyone in that area looked, suspect. However, she pushed this to the back of her mind and focused on her goal. She passed English but failed in Math. On the last day of college, she decided to re-visit the hostel where her mum had stayed. She asked a few people if they knew the hostel and was pointed in the right

Briyell Jones

direction. After a 15-minute walk, she eventually found it. She pressed the buzzer and waited to be let in.

A slender white lady was sitting at reception. She gave the lady her mums name and asked if any possessions of hers were still there. 'No!' she answered coldly. 'I knew her,' a man interjected 'she lived here for a little while, but I'm afraid we don't have anything of hers still here,' he replied. Disheartened but still driven, Briyell asked to see the tree where her mother's ashes were scattered. He guided her to it; it stood tall as it did four years ago. Briyell cried a river but eventually pulled herself together, thanked the man for assisting her and left with mixed emotions.

Conversations with Grandma

2001

TODAY BRANDON AND BRIYELL VISITED THEIR GRANDMA. SHE WELCOMED them and gave them something to eat. Brandon switched on the TV, and they tuned into a talk show. The episode was based on adults wanting to know why they had been placed in care as a child. Throughout the show, Briyell's mind raced about her own childhood and that of her fathers. She plucked up the courage to ask her gran about the reason she sent her dad to live in Barbados as an infant. She explained that she was the eldest of two sisters, she was living with her mum, whilst her youngest sister had left home and got married. She decided to stay home as she loved being looked after. She went on to say that her other sister later moved to England and sent for her. She thought it was a good idea until she remembered she had limited life skills as her mother had always looked after her. She said when she arrived in England, she cried and cried because of her lack of self-sufficiency.

Three years later, she revealed she got pregnant and was angry about this. 'I don't regret having my son, but I was an angry person. I argued and argued until I drove his dad away to another woman'. Eventually, she met someone new, but they also argued a lot which she said her son hated. She explained that their dad attended school but would often play truant. She said she could not remember exactly when or even if he had finished school. She would tell him that he needed to move forward in

Briyell Jones

life and pressed him to work. 'I'm not working for any white man' was his reply. She laughed, threw her head back and said, 'it's the white man that's going to pay you, I worked two jobs in this country, and the white man paid me very well!'. She said her son was ignorant and liked to do his own thing, so she left him to it. She said he started dating women but had very little information about this subject.

The conversation then turned to drugs. 'Drugs is a very serious thing, and if you don't know what you're doing, you get into trouble. Maybe one day you make a £10, the next day a £20, but you nuh know if you ago mek fi si £30, it was a serious ting'. Briyell knew she was referring to her dad being sent to prison. 'If it weren't for Joy, I wouldn't have even seen that place.' 'What a life, what a life!' she said and sighed. Briyell was grateful her grandma had told her as much as she could about her life and how she felt at the time. She understood her reasons for not looking after her dad but still thought she could have done more.

A few years prior, Briyell and Brandon's grandma were called to a family meeting regarding their placement. She was asked if she could look after them long-term until something came up. She laughed, picked up her bag and said, 'grannies got to go now,' she flung her jacket on and walked out the door! She did, however, have them over some weekends. One morning Briyell heard her on the phone, 'Yes, Laurel is an angel,' she said, referring to her eldest granddaughter, 'and the two devils are upstairs, yes man, they're devils, I tell you.' Briyell laid there thinking how she could say such a thing. She thought grandparents were supposed to love their grandchildren regardless. They did have issues but to be compared to the devil himself was something else. Briyell was bitter for years about this, but now knowing that her grandmother had no understanding of how to be a mother, she forgave her.

During half term, Joy rang Briyell out of the blue and told her she would be renewing her wedding vows in Paris and bought a ticket for her to attend. Briyell thanked her and apologised for the misunderstanding

In Search of Self

they had. The flight did not take long, and when the plane landed, everybody clapped and cheered. The week was jam-packed with fun activities, and they enjoyed a few delicacies whilst soaking up the sun. Briyell visited a few landmarks with her family members and had an awesome time with them. Joy and her husband renewed their vows, and the celebration was spectacular! When Briyell arrived back in the UK, Brandon came around to her flat. She showed him pictures from the holiday and immediately he got angry and started trashing the place. 'How comes *I* didn't get to go?' he yelled. She explained it might have been due to his behaviour over the years as to why he did not go. 'But we're twins, wherever you go, I should go, if you get a flat, then I should get a flat, that's how it should be,' he continued. She did not know if he was wrong or right. One thing she did know was that she was tired of being on the receiving end of his angry outbursts. However, she just had to deal with it.

Baby Talk

HALFWAY THROUGH THIS, BRIYELL LEARNT THAT HER BROTHER WOULD soon become a father. Joy had met with him and asked about the situation and who this young lady was. He told her that she was his girlfriend and that her name was Nya. Joy arranged to meet them both to understand more of the situation and later took them to meet Brandon's dad, where they spoke further. Everyone exchanged numbers, and support was there if they needed it.

Briyell laid awake in bed one night; her phone rang, and she answered it. 'Nya ah have a baby right now!' her dad shouts. Her heart skipped a beat, like the one she heard in the background. She laughed and thought, 'some things never change'. She called Brandon and their younger sister to tell them the news; They met and got a lift to the hospital. In the labour ward, Briyell asked a nurse to guide them to the right room. Standing outside the door, Briyell turned to her brother and scowled, 'you should have been here hours ago'. As they enter, Briyell clocked eyes with a person she recognised. A lady who she once worked alongside. 'Hi Doreen', Briyell said, surprised. 'Hi, Briyell, is *this your* brother?' she asks with annoyance in her tone. 'Yes', she countered, and tension filled the room. Doreen was Nya's mum. 'It really is a small world', she thought.

Briyell looked at her new-born nephew in the arms of his mother, and tears filled her eyes. 'He resembles his dad', she thought and imagined what Brandon must have looked like when he was born. She got emotional and left the room. 'How can you just leave a new-born baby by himself!' she spat to herself. Her childhood started creeping back to her. In hindsight, it should not have been about her or her issues, but she could not help it. She was happy to have a beautiful nephew and was sympathetic to Nya as she saw that she was still fragile from giving birth. This was the first time she had met her and her family. Briyell, Brandon, and their sister were the only ones on their side of the family. A surge of heat shot from under Briyell's collar as Nya's aunt turned to her and said, 'It sounded like your dad was in a dance when we spoke to him'. The truth is, he was, and it bothered Briyell. He should have made his way to the hospital as soon as he found out.

Brandon held his son, and Briyell took pictures. Love filled the room, and that was all that mattered. A while later, Joy arrived and was greeted by Nya's family. At least she showed up at the hospital, which was more than Briyell could say for her dad. Even though Brandon had missed his son's birth, he played an active role in his sons' life and visited him regularly. He would financially support them and occasionally pick him up from primary school. Even when he was confined either in prison or in hospital, he always ensured that contact was made and that he saw his son; Briyell's side of the family arranged this; they would rotate the visits and have him over some weekends. It just so happened that over the year's things became difficult for Brandon; issues around his housing, health and well-being were a major factor. He found it difficult to manage from day to day, which eventually impacted his relationship with his family.

The Break-In

At work, Briyell received a call from a neighbour. 'Briyell, somebody just broke into your yard!' he bellowed. She informed her manager, who permitted her to leave. When she arrived at the scene, the door had been kicked off the hinges. She entered the house, scanned the room, and noticed her purse and Nintendo Wii was missing and immediately knew who the culprit was. The police took a statement, and the forensic team did their thing. She felt angry and found it hard to trust as the person responsible was the closest person she knew. There was a range of other problems going on around the flat that weighed heavy on her mind. She was stressed and needed change. She spoke to a friend about what had happened, and the conversation changed to her dreams and aspirations. One of which was singing. He told her his cousin was looking for a new band member and encouraged her to go to the studio, but she pondered and procrastinated.

Weeks later, Brandon turned up at her flat, asking for money that she did not have. He lost his temper and started trashing the place. Her phone then rang. She answered, and it was one of the guys from the studio asking if she was available to come down. She explained the situation and told him that she could not make it. She was sure that he heard the shouting in the background and advised her that whatever she was going through needed to be dealt with as it was only holding her back. Brandon was now in a fit of rage. Trembling, she asked him to leave, but he would not. She needed a fast escape! 'Okay, let us go

In Search of Self

to a cash point!' she shouted, and immediately he calmed down. Once outside, she locked her door and dashed down the road. He bolted after her, and she ran into a shop for safe keeping. 'I thought you were going to a cash point!' he shouted. 'I don't have any money,' she cried back. His eyes were red, and the veins in his neck stuck out. He looked desperate! 'Get out of my shop, or I will call the police!' the shopkeeper yelled. She ran out, with him in tow behind her. She took out her phone, but he grabbed it and threw it into the middle of the road. Cars zoomed by, but luckily, she was able to get it. Her adrenaline was pumping, and her hands were shaking. She dialled her dad and told him what was going on. 'You can't get a brick or something and burst his head!' she told him she would get arrested if she took his advice, and he said he could not help. She felt alone, vulnerable and scared with no one around to help.

She went through her phone book and dialled the producer, who supposedly lived on the same road. He answered. Panting through the phone, she explained the situation and told him her whereabouts. Minutes later, a man in his late forties approached them. He sees Brandon's aggression towards Briyell, grabs his clothing and tells him he has no right to treat her like that. Brandon shouts, 'who are you, bruv, and how do you know my sister?' To Briyell, his question was irrelevant as she would have just got beat down if it were not for this guy. She went back to his house, which had a studio setup and explained to him what happened. 'If you want to find peace, then you need to get rid of all the people that cause you harm', was his advice. Before she left, they arranged a time and date for her to audition. On the audition day, she nervously made her way to the studio, pressed the buzzer, and waited to be let in. The producer introduced her to the lead singer. They told her to make herself comfortable and to sing when she was ready. She sang a well-known song and was given constructive criticism and was accepted into their band.

Escapism

At University, she worked hard on her essays which were not easy, but nothing in life is! She had joined forces with the guys at the studio and was becoming more confident in herself. She attended the studio two days a week whilst studying and working part-time. She would visit her niece and nephew and enjoyed spending time with them. Although her past had been full of ups and downs, she knew things would get better. Her aim for this year was to establish emotional growth. To accept the things, she could not change and change the things she could.

Weeks later, Brandon was arrested and sent to prison. Briyell was deeply saddened for him. When she visited him, it bought back memories of visiting her parents in jail as a child. She hated the fact that he got arrested, but on the other hand, she had peace of mind knowing he was off the streets and would not be around to harass her for money, food, or things to sell, but she missed him dearly. A few months later, he was released from prison, and his constant harassment became worse. He needed professional help, and Briyell could not help him any more than she already had. During half-term, she decided to book a holiday to Spain for the week and did not tell anyone she was going. She figured no one would miss or even notice she was gone. It was all a part of the journey of emotional growth in which she was seeking.

In Spain, on the coast of Costa-Del-Sol, sun, sea, and sand was all she could think about. Most importantly, she had time to relax.

In Search of Self

The sun blazed 24/7, the people were welcoming, and the view from the hotel was beautiful. She saw trees that bore fruit and marvelled at the livestock walking freely around. She glimpsed the nightlife and entertainment and took time to write down some meaningful things for herself. She even brought some coursework to complete in the hotel. Each day was complete bliss. Though she had no idea where she was at times, people could always point her in the right direction. On the third day, a carnival was in full swing. She took a stroll to see the excitement. She could hear loud music; people roaring from the crowds and saw people in fancy dress costumes. She walked around to see if she could ask someone about the history of the event. There were people who had no idea what she was asking them; instead, they looked at her puzzled and shrugged their shoulders. Eventually, she stumbled across students like herself who told her that it was a celebration of different cultures. She was really surprised to see a group of girls in fancy dresses with pillows under their skirts dolling blackface. It was a kodak moment. 'Snap' went her camera as she captured the ignorant and racist act. She stayed a while longer and returned to her hotel as it was the safest thing to do. The next morning, she went out and came across a secluded area. The view was breath-taking. She sat down and took in the sight. An hour later, she was joined by a few young people around the same age as her. The leader of the pack had a bag in his hand; he opened it and shouted 'cogollo', which meant 'bud' in Spanish. As he shared it out, his crew roared like lions. He looked at Briyell and asked if she smoked; she said 'si', and he handed her some. She stayed put for a few hours and spoke with a few of the girls there. She did not realise how similar these young people were to her in the UK. Unemployment, drugs, crime, and poverty were all factors experienced by these young people. She knew these things existed worldwide but never knew the effects until she experienced them for herself. Unfortunately, her time here was

Briyell Jones

running out. It was soon time to go back to the stress, which she had temporally escaped.

Back in the UK, things were no different to when she had left. She had the weekend to finish planning her essay, caught up with some friends, and shared her holiday experience. University, on the other hand, was more challenging than ever. She totally isolated herself from friends and family during her studies as she thought it would help her focus. She managed to hand her essays in on time and just had to wait for her results. This was always a nerve-racking time of year, but thankfully, she passed her second year. She was thrilled and was full of hopes and dreams of becoming successful. She finally understood the message her math teacher had written in her leaving book, 'Education is the ladder to success, climb it', and this was what she intended to do.

Hit-and-Miss

2003

BRIYELL'S WORLD CRASHED WHEN SHE GOT A CALL FROM THE POLICE explaining her brother had been arrested and sent to Prison for a string of offences. Disheartened, she made a few calls regarding visitation. Inside the visiting room, Brandon told her the reason for his arrest. She gave him her thoughts and reassured him that he would be fine. Briyell looked around at the other prisoners and their families. Some women were dolled up for their partners and saddened parents with remorse in their eyes, and it must have been hard to see their child in jail. On the other side of the room, people were queuing for the tuck shop. She joined the line, bought a few refreshments, and went back to sit with Brandon. He told her that he missed his son and that the mother would occasionally visit him, which lifted his spirits. They spoke a little longer, and eventually, time was up. They hugged and said their goodbyes, and as Briyell walked away, she started to cry but told herself he was safe and that she did not need to worry, though she still did.

Months had passed, and Briyell was now entering her third year of university, where the real work began. She was sitting in one of her favourite lectures, jotting down some notes, when her phone rang. It was the police who told her that Brandon had been admitted to a Mental Health hospital. Immediately she felt deflated. She had been learning about Mental Health in one of her lectures and thought it was no place

Briyell Jones

for him to be. 'Or could it have been?' she thought. She phoned the hospital and booked a visit. 'Don't take the medication!' she blurted out when she saw him. She knew that they would have administered it to 'calm him down.' She hated the fact that he was there, but he reassured her that he was okay and that he preferred it to prison. Every week she visited and brought him Sunday dinner. She soon noticed he was getting bigger and no longer looked like the brother she knew. His breathing became heavier, and he would be out of breath by the time he walked from his room to the visiting area. He would complain of exhaustion within minutes of seeing her. She expressed her concerns and fought with them to lower his medication dosage and called her dad to ask for his support. Each week she asked Brandon if their dad had visited, and the answer was always no. This angered her, and she knew it affected Brandon. Every son needs his father, but things were no different compared to when they needed him as children. She was her brother's keeper, and it had always been that way!

Her relationship with Joy was non-existent, and they had not spoken since she moved into her flat. One Mother's Day Briyell, decided to visit Joy at work. She bought her a card and wanted to apologise for their misunderstanding. She nervously made her way to Joy's office and saw her sitting at her desk. 'What you doing here?... I don't want to see you. Have you forgotten the way you disrespected me? After all, I had done for you, even when your mom and dad did nothing for you! You will never live to see me again, as a matter of fact, I feel like moving far away from you as possible, so you will never find us again. You mean nothing to me!' she yelled in one breath. Her words stabbed Briyell in the heart, and she was in indescribable pain. Joy told her to sit down, and she did. Another lady was present, and Joy began telling her about Briyell's life. Briyell stood up and said, 'I'm not going to let you embarrass me in front of a stranger!' and backed out of the room. With her back against the cold wall, she slid down, crying uncontrollably. It

In Search of Self

was hard to stand, but she eventually found her feet; she stumbled down the stairs and went home crying all the way.

Years later, Joy found it in her heart to forgive Briyell. She invited her to her house and went thinking all was well. Joy had guests over when she arrived, so Briyell went into Joys daughters' room and spent some time with her. She then called Briyell from the hallway, and she awkwardly walked towards her. 'This is Briyell', the facety one I was telling you about, and she doesn't have any manners! ´ She spat to one of her guests. Briyell looked to the floor in embarrassment. 'Yeah, man, she continued; she doesn't have any respect for me, dis little gal!'. 'Why did I come here to get humiliated' thought Briyell, unsure where to put herself.

A few weeks later, Briyell cheered herself up by taking some professional photos. She packed a bag with her best clothes and took the train to the make-over studio. She was offered a glass of buck fizz on arrival. A tall white lady called her over and introduced her to a black lady who did her hair and makeup. Briyell looked in the mirror and is pleasantly surprised. She thanks her then heads upstairs to the photographers. The studio is buzzing. She changes into her first outfit; the photographer told her to relax and coaxed her all the way through. The session lasted for an hour or so. She felt like a star but guess that was the whole point. After a lengthy wait, she was called by an over-enthusiastic lady who told her she looked great in all the photos. She selected an album, agreed on a price, then headed home.

At university, the workload had increased, and Briyell was busting her brain to complete deadlines. With her student loan, she bought a new bed, sofa, TV and a new sound system for her flat. She was a little house proud until one evening she noticed mouse droppings all over the kitchen and immediately freaked out! She began to clean frantically and ensured there was no food left for the mice to have a party with. She could not cook until it was sorted. The next day she called pest

Briyell Jones

control; they came and placed mice traps around the flat. Every so often, she would hear them scuffling from room to room. She thought about Michael Jackson and his pet mouse Ben to keep calm, but these mice were not going to be her pet. They needed to go! She ate microwaved meals and was not eating as she should have been and started losing weight. There was also a case of damp growing in the flat that was spreading like ivy. It was enough to make anyone sick! There were also a few burglaries by troubled youths, and days before a raid had been carried out a few doors down from her, Briyell decided to write to the council explaining her difficulties at this address. Enough was enough!

She was home studying one evening, and something did not feel right. She opened her front door and randomly cursed something out. A minute after, four youths came rushing out of her neighbour's house, and her neighbour ran out frantically screaming, 'Briyell, Briyell, you just saved my life, she was shaking hysterically. She stammered 'they, they, they broke into my house. I was in the toilet; they had a gun to my face asking for money and food. I told them I only had milk and rice'. Briyell tried to calm her down and explained that they meant drugs and money. They called the police, who came and took a statement. The neighbour told Briyell she no longer felt safe living in her flat and asked to stay with her for a while. Briyell said yes, and her neighbour got re-housed a few weeks after. 'What about me?' Briyell thought as she was still battling with her housing issues. She no longer felt safe and decided to write to the local MP, but nothing was done.

The Breakdown

2004

At university, Briyell was introduced to critical analysis. Her mind became more critical and analytical in the worst way. She was researching like crazy. She stopped eating meat, watching TV and found it hard to listen to music without thinking about the lyrics and content of the songs. She was 'losing it', 'tripping', 'going mad', some would say. A close friend's grandmother also died of cancer that year and having not dealt with death since her late mother; she never thought it would have impacted her the way it did. She was deeply saddened for the family, and it felt like she was grieving all over again.

At this time, she was casually dating and found it did more harm than good, and, through this experience, she was unfortunately raped. She felt ashamed about this and thought she was partly to blame. She was smoking a lot more than usual, which also impacted her perception of things. She reached out to a family member for help with the ongoing issues in her flat and told them all that was bothering her. At the end of the conversation, Briyell was advised to book a doctor's appointment. Inside the doctor's office, she offloaded everything on her mind. The doctor suggested she was in a bad place and diagnosed her with anxiety and depression; referred her to a psychologist and prescribed her anti-depressants.

Briyell grew even more anxious now that she had been diagnosed;

she beat herself up and asked herself how she got to this point. She thought about the university and how she would complete her final year in this state. She went back to her doctors and asked them to write a letter explaining her difficulties and need to take a year out. This was the hardest decision she had to make; she rattled her brain whether to put her studies on hold or quit completely. When depressed, it is hard to make rational decisions. It took her a good while to know what she wanted to do, and, in the end, she put her studies on hold. With all of this going on, she felt unloved, unwanted, and useless. Guilt consumed her; she knows she had made some wrong decisions but could not shift this feeling for a long time. She was advised to read a few influential and encouraging books, including the Bible, and over time it helped eliminate some of the guilt but ultimately, she had to get herself out of this frame of mind. She received counselling and slowly began doing the things she did before the breakdown.

2005

A year and so had passed, and she was in much better health and shape. She returned to the university and would be graduating later that year. She reunited with friends and family and enjoyed socialising again. She was well in need of a holiday and thought about going to Barbados to see her family. Around this time, she was introduced to a man who also lived in Barbados. They spoke for hours every day and eventually formed a long-distance relationship. Marriage came up, and they both decided that it was something they wanted to do. Both mothers approved, so all Briyell had to do was get her dad's blessing which he half-heartedly gave. She booked the flight, and her soon to be husband met her at the airport. He lived independently, which she admired as it showed he could look after himself. They had much in common and got on well. They had to adapt to each other quite

In Search of Self

quickly. It was not easy, but life experiences had served to build her character and how to be in a relationship. They visited each other's family and friends and were counselled to some extent about marriage. Her cousin had married a month before them and was also in Barbados with her husband. Together they planned days out and enjoyed each other's company. Briyell got married, had a wonderful ceremony, and the honeymoon was blissful. This was by far one of the best moments in her life. Prior to meeting her husband, she had not been in a stable relationship and had looked for love in all the wrong places and suffered to some degree because of it. Had she known the importance of God's love in her life and had stuck to his word, many of the heartbreaks she experienced could have been avoided.

A New Lease of Life

2006

SUNDAY MORNING, BRIYELL AROSE FROM SLUMBER AND STAGGERED INTO the bathroom to shower. Her skin felt sensitive to the water, and she realised that she had missed her period. Immediately she called Joy and told her about the symptoms she felt. 'You're pregnant!' she shrieked and advised her to buy a pregnancy test. Briyell became anxious, and her mind raced. Eventually, she plucked up the courage and bought a pregnancy test. Within that time, Joy rang and asked if she had done the test, and Briyell told her she was in the process. 'Run the tap and sit on the toilet...don't hang up; I want to hear', she said. Briyell laughed and told her she would call her with the results. An hour later, she had them. She washed her hands and went into the kitchen where her husband was. 'I'm pregnant, we're pregnant,' she shouted in excitement. He looked at her, smiled, and they hugged. They told Joy; she cried and congratulated them. Her husband's mum was equally excited. It was a new lease of life!

Briyell enjoyed most of her pregnancy except the morning sickness that crept up in the third month. She went off meat completely but maintained a healthy diet throughout. She took progression photos, downloaded a range of baby apps and kept updated on the weekly developmental stages. She was thrown a wonderful, surprise baby shower in the eighth month and was excited as the baby was a month

In Search of Self

away. Her husband supported her throughout her whole pregnancy. He gave her regular massages, cooked dinner, made her smoothies, helped clean the house and treated her like a china doll, gentle and fragile.

At 36 weeks, she packed up from work and had a good send-off. Her colleagues showered her with gifts which she was grateful for. She now had time to rest and focus on the baby's arrival. She washed and organised her baby's clothes and made sure to have all the essentials. At this point, she was now 40 weeks pregnant and ready to have the baby but was four days overdue. When the baby finally came, Briyell cried tears of joy; the baby was cleaned up and handed to her. Briyell cried even more as she held her baby close. She never wanted to let her go. Hours later, Briyell realised something significant about the date her baby was born but could not put her finger on what it was exactly. She put it to the back of her mind and thought she would figure it out when she got home. In the meantime, her family and her husband's visited the hospital and basked over the baby. A few days later, they were discharged to go home. Briyell placed the baby in her Moses basket and decided to check her mother's death certificate; at that very moment, the baby cried out in her sleep. This startled Briyell, who then walked over to the baby and covered her in prayer. She stirred then fell back to sleep. Briyell went back over to read the certificate, and it confirmed what she subconsciously knew. Her baby was born on the same day as her mother's death 12 years ago. Briyell grew anxious but theorised that a day of mourning would now be a day of celebration.

The Calling

AT THREE MONTHS, THE BABY WAS CHRISTENED, AND DURING THE ceremony, Briyell had learnt a great deal. One is that although she had birthed a beautiful baby girl, she was not solely hers. She was God's child. Briyell thought about how to possibly raise her to know Christ if she did not know him herself. One of the requirements was to turn away from all things that were not pleasing to God and draw closer to him. She had already given up the bad habit of smoking and had long stopped lying and stealing. It was not easy but reflecting on her own life helped her through it. She had to break the cycle! Months later, she kept hearing a voice saying come, come, come, she ignored it and thought it would go away, but it did not. God was calling her! Eventually, she could no longer ignore his call and decided to attend church one Sunday. The service was great, and she felt blessed afterwards. Weeks later, she was invited to the church's convention, and as the word was spoken, she was converted. She nervously made her way to the pulpit and was ministered to; she repeated the sinner's prayer and gave her life to Jesus. She attended church every Sunday and enjoyed it. She soon learnt that there would be a baptism service and signed herself up.

2007

Today would be a day that she would not forget! A new beginning. The day she would be born again, baptised in the name of the Father, the Son,

In Search of Self

and the Holy Spirit. She woke up feeling good, made some cornmeal porridge, ate, and got ready for church. Her husband dropped them off, and she thanked and kissed him goodbye. They entered the church and were warmly welcomed. The morning service was great; the pastor briefly explained the baptism class and encouraged everyone to make it back for the ceremony. Before this, she had been attending a class for new Christians to learn more about their faith. She also had a few meetings with the pastor about the purpose of baptism and its meaning.

Evening fell upon them, and Briyell was downstairs preparing for baptism. She was dressed in white alongside eight other candidates, her nerves grew. They sat together and went through the process of how the ceremony would go. They were numbered and told to sit accordingly. The first half took part upstairs. Each candidate gave testimony about why they were getting baptised. Briyell mentioned she had grown up in church and was in and out throughout her adolescence, and now, as an adult, she would choose to take her faith seriously. She had decided that there was nothing in the world for her. God was all she needed, and He was most important. The baptism took place downstairs. One by one, they made their way into the pool. The pastor spoke with each of them, and they chose a victory song to get baptised too. Briyell chose her song and was instructed by the Pastor to join her hands; he held onto them and submerged her into the water. When she arose, everyone clapped and cheered. Immediately after, she felt different.

The weight that she had been carrying for years was lifted; she was happier and felt brand new. She received some lovely gifts and no longer felt the need to search for anything other than what she had found, her identity in Jesus Christ! She knew that her Christian walk would not be easy, but she would stand strong in her faith by God's grace. Years later, in all that she had learnt and was still learning about the Christian faith, she no longer felt alone, isolated or rejected. This was one of Gods promises to her, that he would never leave or forsake her. As she read

Briyell Jones

her Bible and spent time with God, she grew spiritually. She spoke to God about things she struggled with, and he helped her navigate her way through them. She no longer held onto things or people who weighed her down. She understood that her talents were a gift from God and that he expected her to use them to honour and glorify him. There was one thing, however, which she struggled with, and that was fear. She had to dig deep, pray, fast, and ask God to remove the spirit of fear from her life. She joined a few ministries within the church, took part in some praise and worship sessions and enjoyed ministering with other great singers. As her passion continued to grow, she continued to seek a deeper connection with God by reading his word, spreading the gospel, and building her relationship with him daily.

Briyell thought about her brother and him still being caught up in the world but continued to pray for his recovery. He had been arrested again this year and was sent to another Mental Health hospital. There was nothing she could do but accept this. She knew he needed professional help, and help is what he would get. The fact that she was now married and had a new-born child was her number one priority. She could no longer rush to visit him in the hospital every weekend, but it was always good when she did. Their relationship now was better than it had ever been. Briyell understood that though they had been through similar things, his journey was completely different from hers. He passed through a system that considered his needs and now managed to co-operate and deal with this process. He has come a long way and worked hard by accepting his past and moving on from it with the help of the mental health professionals involved in his care. Briyell now accepts that he has suffered a history of mental health and needed intervention for this. She continues to keep in touch with him regularly and encourages him to take his medication as it is needed for his recovery.

Briyell's experiences through the care system enabled her to build up resilience, which helped her cope with the situations she was put in.

In Search of Self

As a child and teenager, she had many anger issues towards her parents, particularly for their absence and inconsistency in her life. She was made to grow up a lot faster than her peers and had to be responsible from an incredibly young age. However, the fact that she had experience living with a family on a long-term basis and then eventually with her biological dad gave her security, despite the challenges within the placements. The older she got, she dreamt of having and becoming more than what was statistically proven about children in care. The more educated she became and the more skills she acquired, she knew what she was willing to accept and the things she wouldn't, especially when it came to breaking life cycles. She knew she didn't want to go down the same road as her biological mother, so she did everything to avoid that. She sometimes felt that if her mother had half of the experience, she had in terms of having a long-term carer there to support and encourage her, then maybe her life would have turned out differently. She now uses those skills to look after her own family. Her faith has a big part to play in her life. Also, she knew that God was the centre of some, if not all, marriages, and without him, things would fail. She wanted to bring her children up as God-fearing, just as she had been. Learning about what happened to her and writing about it has been a huge part of her healing process. Putting into perspective and understanding her parents' background was an essential part of her healing process. It gave her an understanding of the struggles they faced and its impact on their ability to parent, and she felt they did the best they could, knowing what they knew at the time. Now, as a young black woman, Briyell has a full understanding of whom she is, where she came from and her purpose in life. She passed many of the things she was taught growing up onto her children, and her faith has been a major part of this. The Bible speaks of ways a child should be bought up, and she believes this to be true. In all she had been through, seeds had been planted; whether she knew it or not, God was always there protecting her.

'In search of self' is a narrative of a young woman searching for identity and belonging. A sense of abandonment leaves her asking the big question, 'who Am I?'. She recounts her life from birth, where she was left in the care system and had to adapt to the stigma of being abandoned. She discusses the issues and challenges faced growing up in an urban society from childhood to adulthood. Despite her struggles, she tries to remain strong and speaks of the beauty of life, her family, friends, and God who have kept her going.

Ingram Content Group UK Ltd.
Milton Keynes UK
UKHW010609070623
423005UK00003B/66